EDGE
BOOKS

The Unexplained

Near-Death Experiences

by **Michael Martin**

Consultant:
Linda Jacquin
Boardmember
International Association for Near-Death Studies
East Windsor Hill, Connecticut

Capstone
press

Mankato, Minnesota

Edge Books are published by Capstone Press
151 Good Counsel Drive, P.O. Box 669, Mankato, Minnesota 56002
www.capstonepress.com

Library of Congress Cataloging-in-Publication Data
Martin, Michael, 1948–
    Near-death experiences / by Michael Martin.
        p. cm.—(Edge books. The unexplained)
    Includes bibliographical references and index.
    Contents: The mystery of near-death experiences—History of NDEs—
Investigating NDEs—Looking for answers.
    ISBN 0-7368-2719-6 (hardcover)
    1. Near-death experiences—Juvenile literature. [1. Near-death experiences.]
I. Title. II. Series.
BF1045.N4M375 2005
133.9'01'3—dc22   2003024298

Editorial Credits
Carrie A. Braulick, editor; Juliette Peters, designer; Kelly Garvin, photo researcher;
    Eric Kudalis, product planning editor

Photo Credits
Art Resource, NY/Scala, 11
Corbis, 12 (door, doll face); ER Productions, 14; George B. Diebold, 25;
    Images.com/Kevin Belford, 5; Patrik Giardino, 22
Creatas, 27 (top)
DigitalVision, 27 (bottom); Jim Reed, 29
Fortean Picture Library/Philip Panton, cover; William Blake, 19
Getty Images Inc./AFP/Rose M. Prousser, 16; Time Life Pictures/Rich Frishman, 21
Index Stock Imagery/Jim McGuire, 9
KGO-TV, 6
Stockbyte, 12 (key)
Susan Blackmore, 23

1 2 3 4 5 6 09 08 07 06 05 04

Table of Contents

Chapter 1

The Mystery of Near-Death Experiences

Millions of people have watched Spencer Christian on TV. For 13 years, he gave weather reports on the ABC show *Good Morning America*. In 1999, he joined KGO-TV in San Francisco. Christian's reports help viewers make plans based on the weather. Most viewers don't know that Christian almost didn't live to become a weather reporter.

Learn about:
• Spencer Christian
• NDE reports
• NDE similarities

People who have had a near-death experience often report visions. These visions may include people.

▲ Spencer Christian had an NDE when he was a child.

Christian was 5 years old when he went to the hospital to have his tonsils removed. Something went wrong during the operation. Christian began bleeding heavily. At one point, doctors feared he would die.

Christian later said he felt like he was floating near the ceiling during the operation. He said he could see doctors and nurses working to save his life. Christian said he felt peaceful as he looked at the scene below. He then decided to go back into his body. He woke up in the hospital's recovery room.

Christian recovered from the operation. Several years later, he realized the happenings were part of a near death experience, or NDE.

About NDEs

Millions of people around the world say they have had an NDE. Between 8 and 15 million Americans claim they have had an NDE.

NDEs can occur during or near clinical death. Clinical death happens after a person stops breathing and the heart stops beating. Clinical death usually lasts less than six minutes. People who are clinically dead can be revived. A revived person sometimes reports an NDE.

Reports of NDEs are similar to one another. Many people say they left their bodies during their NDEs. They say they were aware of their surroundings. Many people report moving through a tunnel toward a light. They usually describe the light as warm and loving. Sometimes people report seeing relatives or friends who have died. Other people say they saw visions of their life experiences. Some people have reported seeing religious figures.

Today, NDE reports are much more common than they were in the past. Doctors now have better medical equipment and training. They can revive more people who are clinically dead.

EDGE FACT

People often report hearing peaceful music during their NDEs.

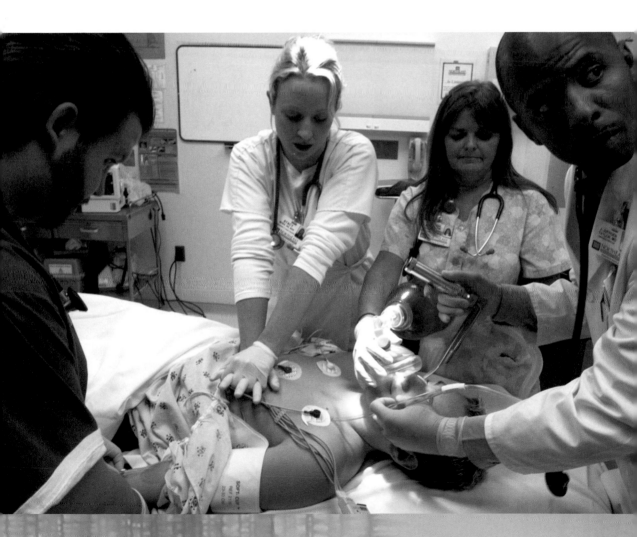

▲ Today's doctors and nurses are able to revive many people who are clinically dead.

Chapter 2

History of NDEs

For thousands of years, people have told stories about NDEs. More than 2,000 years ago, the Greek philosopher Plato wrote a story about a soldier named Er. Er died while fighting in a war. Suddenly, Er's spirit flew up in the air. The spirit traveled to a strange land. The spirits of other dead soldiers traveled with Er. Er was sent back to his body so he could tell others about the new land. Er awoke back in his body.

Learn about:
- An NDE story
- Dr. James Hyslop
- Books about NDEs

Plato wrote a story about a soldier who had experiences similar to those in NDE reports.

11

EDGE FACT

▲ People who have hallucinations may see objects and people.

First Studies and Reports

In 1882, the Society for Psychical Research formed. Researchers in the organization began studying NDEs and other unexplained events.

Dr. James Hyslop studied psychology in the early 1900s. He researched NDEs and memory. Hyslop wrote a famous research paper about NDEs in 1907. In 1919, Hyslop wrote a book called *Contact with the Other World*. He described people's NDE reports in the book.

Early NDE researchers tried to explain NDEs. Dr. Edward Clarke thought NDEs happened when the brain failed to work properly. Other scientists thought NDEs happened when people imagined seeing things that were not really there. This activity is called hallucinating.

In 1943, George Ritchie became very sick while training in the U.S. Army. He was clinically dead for several minutes. After Ritchie awoke, he reported an NDE. His detailed report caused Dr. Raymond Moody to become interested in NDEs. Moody later became a well-known NDE researcher.

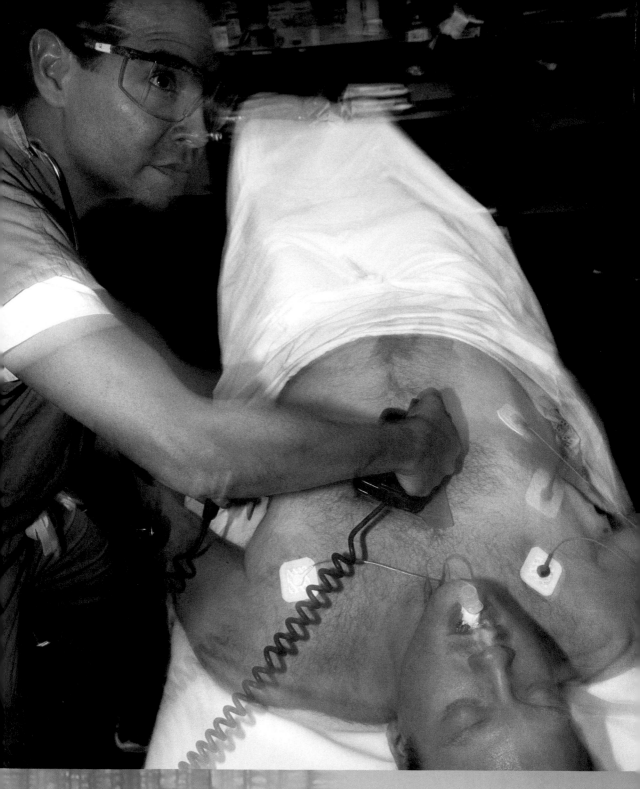

▲ People who have had an NDE sometimes accurately report their surroundings.

Interest in NDEs Grows

In 1969, Dr. Elizabeth Kubler-Ross wrote a book called *On Death and Dying*. It told about the emotions that dying people experience. The book sold millions of copies. The book's popularity caused more scientists to become interested in studying death.

In 1975, Moody wrote a book about NDEs called *Life after Life*. It included 150 NDE stories. One story was about a woman who had been blind since childhood. She had a heart attack and was brought to a hospital. She said she could see the hospital room during her NDE. Her description of the room was correct.

In 1977, NDE researchers Karlis Osis and Erlendur Haraldsson studied NDE reports from people in several countries. They found that many NDE reports were similar.

Sharon Stone's NDE

Actress Sharon Stone has had a near-death experience. In 2001, an artery tore near the base of her head. Her head began bleeding internally. Her husband rushed her to the hospital. Afterward, Stone said she traveled toward a bright light. Stone also said she met some of her friends and relatives who had died. Today, Stone tells others about her experience.

Sharon Stone has talked about her NDE on TV shows.

Other Studies

In 1981, scientists began learning about the effects of cerebral anoxia. This condition occurs when the brain does not receive enough oxygen. Hallucinations can happen when the brain lacks oxygen. Some scientists believe NDEs are caused by cerebral anoxia.

In 1982, Dr. Michael Sabom wrote a book about NDEs. It is called *Recollections of Death: A Medical Investigation*. Sabom noticed that many people accurately reported happenings around them while they were clinically dead.

In 1984, scientists Russell Noyes and Donald Slymen did an NDE study. They wanted to find out if the cause of death affected NDEs. They studied NDEs that happened as a result of falls, automobile accidents, drownings, serious illnesses, and other events. Noyes and Slymen found that more accident and fall victims reported a separation from their bodies than other victims. People who were seriously ill had more visual images and feelings of joy.

Chapter 3

Investigating NDEs

Scientists study different features of NDEs. Some scientists study the similarities among NDEs. Other scientists study the brain to find out what causes NDEs. Each new study can help people understand NDEs better.

NDE researcher Dr. Kenneth Ring identified five stages of NDEs in 1980. Ring believes the first stage is a feeling of peace and happiness. The second stage is a feeling of leaving the body. The third stage is entering a tunnel. The last two stages are seeing a bright light and entering the light.

Learn about:
• Dr. Kenneth Ring
• Effects of NDEs
• Dr. Melvin Morse

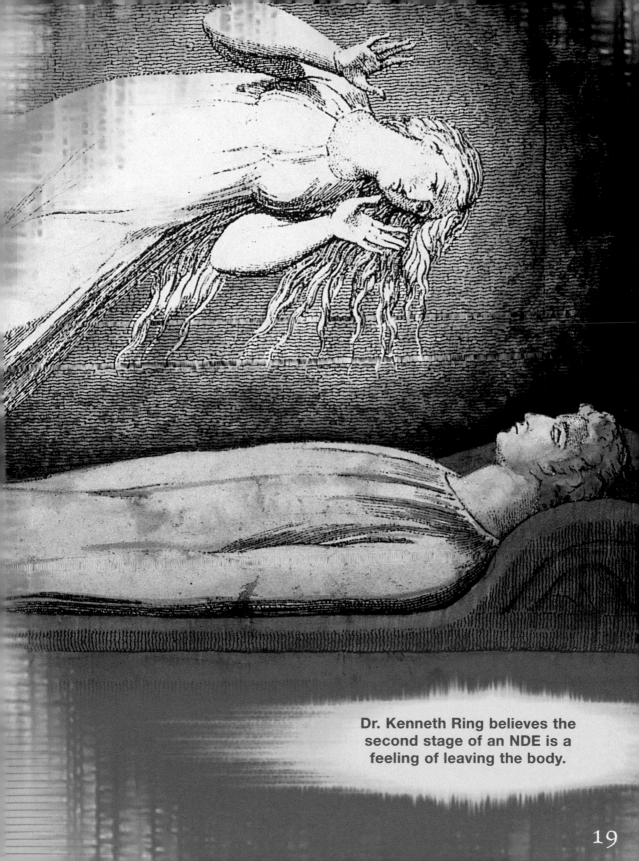

Dr. Kenneth Ring believes the second stage of an NDE is a feeling of leaving the body.

Changed Lives

Some scientists study the effects of NDEs on people's lives. In 1984, Ring found that people who have NDEs become more helpful to others. He said they are less concerned with themselves after an NDE.

In the early 1990s, Dr. Melvin Morse studied NDE effects. Morse chose 100 people who had experienced NDEs as children. He compared them to another group of 250 people. These people had not had NDEs. Morse gave the people several tests. The tests were designed to show feelings about life and death.

Morse found that people view life and death differently after an NDE. The people who had a childhood NDE were less afraid of death than the other people. These people also reported enjoying life more than they did before the NDE.

Susan Blackmore

Many people believe the spirit lives on after the body dies. In 1993, researcher Susan Blackmore studied this belief. She gave reasons why this idea may not be true.

▲ Dr. Melvin Morse has studied the NDE reports
of children.

Common Parts of NDEs

1. A feeling of great happiness, peacefulness, or calmness

2. The feeling of separating from the body and viewing its surroundings from a distance

3. Passing through an area of darkness or a tunnel toward a bright light

4. Meeting objects of light that send out a strong feeling of love

5. Meeting with relatives or friends who have died

6. A review of how one has lived his or her life

7. A feeling of understanding how the universe works

8. A decision or command to return to life

Blackmore wrote a book about her studies called *Dying to Live*. Blackmore says that NDEs may be caused by a dying brain. The book also says hallucinations caused by drugs may be related to NDEs. Both legal and illegal drugs can cause visions.

▼ Susan Blackmore believes NDES may be caused by a dying brain.

Chapter 4

Looking for Answers

NDEs are difficult to study at the time they happen. Almost all information about NDEs comes from personal stories. The reports are hard to measure by scientific methods. Scientists often prove things by doing experiments that can be repeated. Repeating an NDE is almost impossible. In recent years, researchers have found new ways to learn about NDEs.

Veridical NDEs

Veridical NDEs support the belief that people can have awareness far from their bodies. During some veridical NDEs, people can see

Learn about:
- Experiences after NDEs
- NDE explanations
- A recent study

NDE reports are difficult to study as they happen.

events far from their body's location. During other veridical NDEs, people meet dead relatives or friends who give them information. The person finds out the information is true after they are revived.

In 1993, Dr. Kenneth Ring published a famous article about a veridical NDE. A woman had a heart attack. Before she was revived, she felt herself floating outside the hospital. She saw a shoe on a third-floor ledge. When she awoke, the woman told the doctor about the shoe. The doctor found the shoe on the ledge.

An Important Study

In 2001, a large NDE study took place in the Netherlands. Researcher Pim van Lommel led the study. Scientists interviewed 344 people after they had been revived following heart attacks.

The study didn't support several commonly believed causes of NDEs. All patients had lost consciousness when their brains did not receive enough oxygen. Only 18 percent of the patients reported having an NDE. The study showed that cerebral anoxia may not be a cause of NDEs.

Van Lommel's study also didn't support
the idea that NDEs are caused by fear of death.
Most of the heart attacks happened suddenly.
The patients didn't have time to be scared.

▼ Some people who have reported veridical NDEs said
they could see happenings far from their body.

Searching for Proof

Many scientists try to explain NDE reports. Some scientists think they are caused by cerebral anoxia. Other scientists wonder if a dying brain produces chemicals that cause hallucinations. Some scientists believe people mistake visions caused by drugs as NDEs.

Several scientists say NDEs are proof of life after death. They believe people who have reported NDEs have experienced an afterlife.

Scientists have much to learn about NDEs. They will continue to study NDE reports. The studies may someday solve the mystery.

▲ NDEs will remain a mystery until scientists learn
their causes.

Glossary

hallucination (huh-LOO-suh-nay-shuhn)—something seen that is not really there

heart attack (HART uh-TAK)—a failure of the heart to deliver blood to the rest of the body

philosopher (fuh-LOSS-uh-fur)—a person who studies truth, wisdom, knowledge, and the nature of reality

spirit (SPIHR-it)—the invisible part of a person that contains thoughts and feelings; some people believe the spirit leaves the body after death.

tonsils (TON-suhlz)—two flaps of soft tissue that lie on each side of the throat

veridical (vuh-RI-di-kuhl)—truthful and real

Read More

Clark, Jerome. *Unexplained!: Strange Sightings, Incredible Occurrences, and Puzzling Physical Phenomena.* Detroit: Visible Ink, 1999.

Landau, Elaine. *Near-Death Experiences.* Mysteries of Science. Brookfield, Conn.: Millbrook Press, 1996.

Internet Sites

FactHound offers a safe, fun way to find Internet sites related to this book. All of the sites on FactHound have been researched by our staff.

Here's how:

1. Visit *www.facthound.com*
2. Type in this special code **0736827196** for age-appropriate sites. Or enter a search word related to this book for a more general search.
3. Click on the **Fetch It** button.

FactHound will fetch the best sites for you!

Index